PerryScope

1

Feb. 15 to Jul. 28, 2017
13-Articles

Perry Diaz

Published by
TATAY JOBO ELIZES.
Self-Publisher
in 2017, under the
permission and authorization
of PERRY DIAZ,
author and owner of the copyright to this book. The copyright owner can withdraw this permission at his discretion without any objection from Talay Jobo Elizes at any time. Printing of this book is using the present day method of Print-On-Demand (POD) system, where prints will never run out of copies to be available for posterity. The copyright owner is free to republish with other publishers anytime.

ISBN - 13: 978 - 1976511172
ISBN - 10: 1976511178

Contact: job_elizes@yahoo.com
Website: http://tinyurl.com/mj76ccq

Special Note

Articles are arranged in reversed chronology descending from newer dates to older dates

Contents

ooooo

About the Author

Perry Diaz started publishing Balita (Global) as a community newsletter in 1987. Over the years, his commentaries and viewpoints have become increasingly popular with Pinoys in the United States, Philippines and abroad. In 2003, Perry started publishing his opinion articles by the name of Perryscope. Today, Global Balita is a daily-published online culmination of Perryscopes, social commentaries, news and features from a variety of respected sources about Filipinos and all that affect them.

All articles can be read freely online at his website PerryScopes or Global Balita, easily accessible in the internet.

The articles are being archived in printed or hardcopy for posterity under print-on-demand system so that prints will never run out. This will serve all readers, young and old, internet-savvy or not, Filipinos or not, for all generations to come.

To contact Perry Diaz directly, please
***email** perrydiaz@gmail.com.*
For advertising opportunities, please
***email** globalbalita@gmail.com.*

1
Is the 'Ilocos Six' A proxy war?
July 28, 2017

In a major setback for Ilocos Norte Governor Imee Marcos, she failed to secure immediate relief from the Supreme Court (SC) against the House of Representatives' (HOR) inquiry into the Ilocos Norte's alleged misuse of P66.45 million in tobacco excise tax funds.

While the SC did not specifically reject Imee's petition, it was re-raffled since the justice in charge of the case, Associate Justice Diosdado Peralta, recused himself from the case. Interestingly, it was Peralta who administered the oath of office of former first lady Imelda Marcos and her son Ferdinand "Bongbong" Marcos Jr. as Ilocos Norte 2nd District representative and senator, respectively, in 2010. But here's the rub: Peralta is a relative of Ilocos Norte 1st District representative and Majority Leader Rodolfo "Rudy" Fariñas, one of the respondents in the case.

In addition to Peralta, Chief Justice Maria Lourdes Sereno and newly appointed Associate Justice Andres Reyes Jr. inhibited themselves from the case. No reason was given for their recusal.

With the three magistrates inhibiting themselves from the case, there will only be 12 justices who can vote on the case, which would require seven votes for approval of the petition. Does Imee have the support of at least seven justices? The fact that majority of the SC justices voted to allow the re-burial of the remains of the late strongman Ferdinand E. Marcos at the Libingan ng mga Bayani (Heroes' Cemetery), indicates the strong influence of President Rodrigo Duterte on the High Court. The interment of Marcos at the Libingan would certainly help Bongbong in his quest for the presidency. Indeed, Duterte had made it known that Bongbong was his preferred successor. But that was before the "Ilocos Six" scandal erupted, pitting Imee Marcos against Rudy Fariñas.

Associate Justice Diosdado Peralta *administers the oath of office of former first lady Imelda Marcos and her son Ferdinand "Bongbong" Marcos Jr. as Ilocos Norte 2nd District representative and senator, respectively.*

Ilocos Six

Majority Floor Leader Rudy Fariñas and Speaker Pantaleon Alvarez.

The "Ilocos Six" controversy might seem complicated and complex in legal terms; but one can see politics at the crux of the matter. There are two groups of very powerful politicians who are involved in the imbroglio. One group is the powerful Marcos political clan of Ilocos Norte, which is led by the former First Lady and Ilocos Norte 2nd District Representative Imelda Marcos, her daughter Governor Imee Marcos, and her only son, former Senator Bongbong Marcos. The other group is led by a triumvirate of the top HOR leaders consisting of Speaker Pantaleon Alvarez, House Majority Leader Rudy Fariñas, and Surigao del Sur Rep. Johnny Pimentel, chair of the HOR's Committee on Good Government and Public Accountability.

While the Marcos siblings defer to their mother Imelda Marcos, who is used to wielding the power that she and her late husband had during the heyday of their conjugal dictatorship, the HOR triumvirs are political protégés of the "Godfather" in Malacañang, President Rodrigo Duterte. They occupy their high positions because the Godfather placed them there to make sure that he has a grip on the HOR. Although nobody would admit to it, they serve at the pleasure of the Godfather. That is the reality of Philippine politics.

The system of "three independent government branches," as stipulated in the Constitution, doesn't work in Philippine realpolitik. What works is the "padrino" system that we had inherited from the Spanish colonizers. Duterte is the padrino or godfather of the HOR triumvirs.

And by the same token, Imelda Marcos is the padrina or godmother of the Marcos clan.

Now the picture is crystal clear: the "Ilocos Six" is a proxy war between Duterte and Imelda Marcos. But what is not clear is why are they fighting each other when not too long ago they were the best of friends?

There is chatter in the grapevine that the Marcoses and Duterte had a falling out. Speculation is rife that a "broken promise" might have been the cause of their estranged relationship. Well, like they say, "In politics you don't know who your friends or enemies are."

The presidential election is still five years away and loyalty could shift from one side to the other at the drop of a hat. And as usual there would be the balimbings – political opportunists – who would jump sides if it satisfied their own agenda.

Political opportunism

Third generation of Marcoses: Bongbong Marcos, sons, and wife.

In my last column, "The politics behind the Ilocos Six" (July 21, 2017), I wrote: "It's interesting to note that both Imee [Marcos] and [Rudy] Fariñas will be termed out in 2019. Which makes one wonder what their political plans are in the 2019 midterm election? Imee could run for Fariñas' 1st District seat, after all she's now officially a resident of Laoag City, which is in the 1st District. Bongbong's eldest son Sandro is now primed to run for office in the province. Why not the governorship that Imee would be vacating? Bongbong's second son, Joseph Simon would be in a position to run for mayor of Laoag City against incumbent Chevylle Fariñas. And Bongbong's youngest son Vincent would qualify to run against Laoag City's incumbent vice-mayor and Chevylle's husband, Michael Fariñas. That would certainly stack up the cards against the Fariñas clan right in their own backyard.

Duterte vs. Marcos

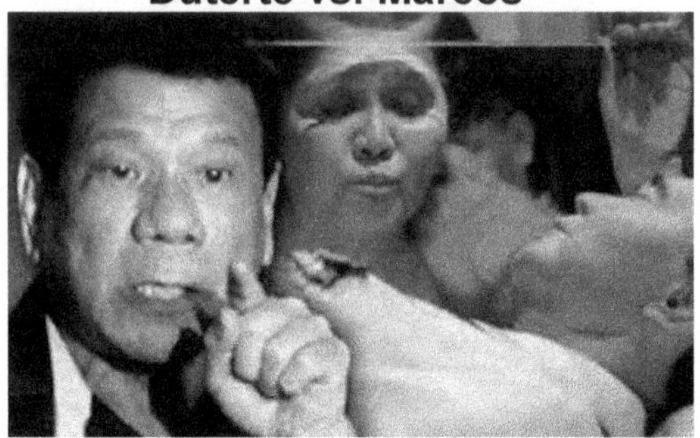

Duterte and Imelda Marcos.

"Meanwhile, Bongbong's electoral protest against Vice President Leni Robredo is now before the Supreme Court convened as Presidential Electoral Tribunal (PET). If

Bongbong wins and takes over the vice presidency, it would certainly make the Marcos clan the preeminent political body in Ilocos Norte. And this could cause the downfall of the Fariñas clan."

With the elimination of the Fariñas clan from the political power structure of Ilocos Norte, Bongbong can then work in securing the support of the Solid North. And with the Visayas and Mindanao getting behind whomever Duterte fronts in 2022, Bongbong is probably salivating right now because he is very confident that he is Duterte's candidate – or as they say in the street, "manok," a fighting cock — in the 2022 presidential election. And he was. What happened?

With the proxy war that is going on between Duterte and Imelda, the calculus for the presidential election in 2022 is going to change. And this begs the question: If Bongbong were not going to be Duterte's candidate, who would it be? Last June, amid speculations about his health, Duterte stressed that Vice President Leni Robredo will be his "only constitutional successor in case his term ends prematurely." Is that a veiled endorsement that Leni could be his anointed successor to the presidency? Why not?

And what's in store for Rudy Fariñas, who has loyally stood by his godfather?

Ooooo

2
The Politics Behind the "Ilocos Six'

July 26, 2017

Imee Marcos vs. Rudy Fariñas.

In Philippine politics, it's hard to determine who the real enemies are. Their enemies today could be their allies tomorrow or vice versa. Which reminds me of Benjamin Disraeli's popular mantra: "We have no permanent friends. We have no permanent enemies. We just have permanent interests." But the Ilocano psyche goes beyond that mantra. To Ilocanos, blood is thicker than water, but politics transcend blood relationships. So don't be misled when brothers face each other in an election. The truth is: no matter who wins, power remains within the family.

And that's to keep others from getting into their "exclusive" domain.

Ortega political clan's centennial, 1901 – 2001.

Take the Ortega political clan for example. They've dominated politics in La Union for the past century. They have occupied the governor's office, won congressional seats and provincial board seats, served as city and town mayors, and sat on city and town councils. They may be running against each other in these elections, but they remain "family."

The Marcoses of Ilocos Norte are now in the same situation. After three generations in politics since World War II, they control the political pendulum in the province. Their patriarch, the late President Ferdinand Marcos, occupied the presidency for more than 20 years.

When the People Power Revolution of 1986 deposed him, the family went into exile in Hawaii. But in the 1990's they were able to come back and eventually, one by one, run for office. Daughter Imee Marcos is now the governor of Ilocos Norte while son Ferdinand "Bongbong" Jr. won a Senate seat; however, he lost in his vice presidential bid last year. The matriarch Imelda Marcos won the 2nd District congressional seat where her late husband began his political career.

In May 2015, Imee officially notified the Commission of Elections that she was a resident of Laoag. In September that same year, the three sons of Bongbong – Ferdinand "Sandro" Alexander III, 23, Joseph Simon, 22, and Vincent, 20 – registered as voters of Laoag City, claiming their dad's house in Barangay Suba as their residence. Imee's youngest son, Matthew Joseph Manotoc, 27, ran for the Ilocos Norte provincial board in 2016 and won.

Three generations of Marcoses: Imelda Marcos, Matthew Joseph Manotoc, and Imee Marcos.

It's interesting to note that Manotoc topped the race edging Ria Christina Fariñas into second place. Ria Christina is Rudy Fariñas' daughter. Manotoc's lead over Ria Christina was of significant importance, which has raised a political red flag in the province. Rudy Fariñas is the patriarch of the powerful Fariñas family that had dominated politics in the 1st District for over half a century.

With the province split into two districts, one controlled by the Fariñas clan and the other by the Marcos clan, the two clans managed to coexist peacefully since the 1980s when the late dictator Ferdinand Marcos ruled the country.

In 1980, Rudy Fariñas, whose family owns and operates Fariñas Trans, one of the oldest fleets of northern Luzon buses, was elected mayor of Laoag, making him one the youngest mayors during his time. In 1988, Fariñas ran for Ilocos Norte governor and won in a landslide. He was reelected in 1992 and 1995. He served as governor for 10 years. After that, he ran and won in 1998 as the 1st District's representative. He served for only one three-year term.

Fariñas' alliance with the Marcoses lasted until 2007 when Fariñas was defeated by a political neophyte, Michael Marcos Keon. Keon was backed by the Marcoses, after all Keon was a first cousin of Imee. But three years later, in 2010, Fariñas and Imee resumed their alliance. Imee tried to stop Keon from running for reelection but Keon wouldn't withdraw. It was then that Imee decided to run against Keon. She won and it prevented the Marcos-Fariñas alliance from disintegrating. However, the alliance didn't last too long.

Ilocos Six

Ilocos Six refuse to answer questions from House committee.

Last year, a scandal erupted in Laoag City over the missing P85 million from the city treasury. The rift between the erstwhile allies, Imee Marcos and Rudy Fariñas, came to a head when the House committee on good government and public accountability started to investigate the alleged misuse of province's tobacco funds in 2012. It was alleged that that P66.4 million worth of buses and multi-cabs were purchased without public bidding.

The House committee summoned six Ilocos Norte officials – called the "Ilocos Six" — to answer questions concerning the missing funds. The officials showed up but they refused to answer questions. This prompted the House committee to order them detained. If they continue to refuse to answer questions, they could be detained until the end of the current Congress in June 2019.

Their boss, Governor Imee Marcos was furious! She lambasted House Majority Floor Leader Fariñas and dared him to bring the fight back to Ilocos Norte. She also sought relief from the Supreme Court. At a press conference, Imee blamed her political rivalry with Fariñas for triggering the House investigation.

Marcos vs. Fariñas

ALLIES TURNED RIVALS. In this photo taken on May 11, 2012, Ilocos Norte 1st District Representative Rodolfo Fariñas joins Governor Imee Marcos in distributing red mini-cabs to barangay captains. (Photo from Governor Imee Marcos)

It's interesting to note that both Imee and Fariñas will be termed out in 2019. Which makes one wonder what their political plans are in the 2019 midterm election? Imee could run for Fariñas' 1st District seat, after all she's now officially a resident of Laoag City, which is in the 1st District. Bongbong's eldest son Sandro is now primed to run for office in the province. Why not the governorship that Imee would be vacating? Bongbong's second son, Joseph Simon would be in a position to run for mayor of Laoag City against incumbent Chevylle Fariñas. And Bongbong's youngest son Vincent would qualify to run against Laoag City's incumbent vice-mayor and Chevylle's husband, Michael Fariñas. That would certainly stack up the cards against the Fariñas clan right in their own backyard.

Meanwhile, Bongbong's electoral protest against Vice President Leni Robredo is now before the Supreme Court convened as Presidential Electoral Tribunal (PET). If Bongbong wins and takes over the vice presidency, it would certainly make the Marcos clan the preeminent political body in Ilocos Norte. And this could cause the downfall of the Fariñas clan.

Ria Christina Fariñas.

Rudy is rumored to be vying to be the next Ombudsman after the retirement of Ombudsman Conchita Carpio-Morales in 2018. Rudy also wants his daughter Ria Christina Fariñas to succeed him in the 1st District in 2019. Ria Christina is currently serving as a Member of the Ilocos Norte Provincial Board. However, she gained some national recognition when she was elected as the new president of the Provincial Board Members League of the Philippines (PBMLP) last February 28.

With Imee terming out in 2019, she might run for a Senate seat. Where else is she going to go? And with Rudy Fariñas terming out too, he might run for a Senate seat. It would certainly be an interesting face-off between the two former allies, now bitter adversaries. Or, Rudy could instead run for governor, which might be easier to win than a Senate seat if Sandro Marcos wouldn't run against him. But there will always be someone from the Marcos camp who would challenge him. Matthew Joseph Manotoc comes to mind. And if he runs, he could give Fariñas a good run for his money.

Which makes one wonder: Is the "Ilocos Six" scandal being used to achieve a political end? Or is it to punish the corrupt?

Machiavelli lives!

Ooooo

3

Who's Behind the Marawi Attack?

July 10, 2017

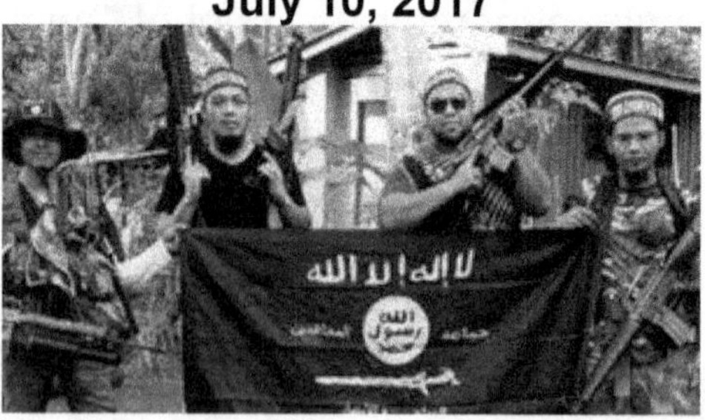

Abu Sayyaf militants show ISIS flag.

Like most rebellions, the Marawi rebellion couldn't have happened without the financial support of someone who has the wherewithal to sustain a long siege. More than six weeks after the attack, the militants are still entrenched in Marawi City. No amount of ground assault by the Philippine Marines or bombing by Philippine Air Force warplanes could dislodge the militants consisting of members of the Maute group and Abu Sayyaf Group (ASG).

Two faces of Abu Sayyaf leader Isnilon Totoni Hapilon.

The Philippine military had been after the ASG terrorists for several years now. Yet, most of the leaders of the ASG managed to evade capture. The most recent one was Isnilon Totoni Hapilon, also known as Abu Abdullah al-Filipini. He is believed to be linked to ISIS. He was formerly leader of ASG before its battalions pledged their allegiance to Abu Bakr al-Baghdadi. An April 2016 issue of ISIS' weekly newsletter Al Naba said that Hapilon had been appointed as *"emir of all Islamic State forces in the Philippines." [Source: Wikipedia]*

Maute leaders (top, left to right): Cayamora Maute, Ominta "Farhana" Romano-Maute, mother of the Maute founders Omar and Abdullah. (Bottom left to right): Maute group members.

What is interesting to note is the role of the Maute matriarch, Ominta "Farhana" Romato-Maute, mother of the Maute founders Omar and Abdullah. Last June 7, she was arrested in Masiu, a town about 34 kilometers from Marawi City, as she and two wounded men and seven women were trying to escape the government troops. She is believed to be the "heart of the Islamic State-inspired Maute group," directing its movement and operations and taking care of finances and international networking. She and her husband Cayamora are said to be the "masterminds" behind the Maute attack. Farhana is reputed to be a "fiercely astute" businesswoman and politician. She manages several business interests including several rental houses in Quezon City, Iligan, Catabato City, and Davao City. She once served as assemblywoman of the Autonomous Region in Muslim Mindanao (ARMM).

Before her capture, Farhana tried calling President Rodrigo Duterte to talk about peace and negotiate a ceasefire after the heavy bombing and fighting in Marawi City. Duterte turned her offer down, saying the government forces have lost too many soldiers in the Marawi attack. The question is: Is Farhana really the mastermind of the Maute group or is someone much higher in the food chain calling the shots?

Farhana's niece Monaliza "Monay" Solaiman Romato.

Last July 5, government forces foiled a possible bombing in Cagayan de Oro when they arrested Farhana's niece Monaliza "Monay" Solaiman Romato. Monay reportedly replaced Farhana as the Maute's matriarch. However, it didn't take too long for the government forces to capture Monay, which begs the question: With Farhana and Monay in detention, who would take over the Maute's financial operations? Or could it be that Farhana and Monay were just figureheads? Is the matriarch's role to shield the real power behind the group? Meanwhile, the real power can lead a normal life conducting his business empire – probably illegal drug trade — out in the open without any fear of scrutiny from the government.

Back-channel talks

President Rodrigo Duterte flanked by AFP Chief of Staff General Eduardo Año (L) and Defense Secretary Delfin Lorenzana (R).

Recently, Reuters reported that President Duterte initiated a move to negotiate an end to the conflict with the Maute group. However, Malacañang said that it has no information on Duterte's reported attempt to hold back-channel talks with the Maute terrorists. The Reuters report said a senior Duterte aide approached Agakhan Sharief, a prominent Muslim leader, to use his connections with the Maute group's leaders to start back-channel talks. The report said the talks failed as the Maute leaders "did not show sincerity and continued to attacks on government forces." Two other sources familiar with the matter confirmed that Duterte had worked behind the scenes to hold talks with the Maute brothers, Omarkhayam and Abdullah. Marawi City Mayor Majul Usman Gandamra also confirmed that back-channel talks were started but said he was not privy to details.

The back-channel talks did not push through when Cayamora was caught on June 6 in Davao City, three days before Farhana's arrest in Lanao del Sur.

Chinese financier

Authorities recovers P10-million worth of shabu from the house of a former Marawi City mayor Omar Solitario Ali last June 23. June 23. Ali is on the list of 125 alleged Maute members ordered arrested by the government. (Credit: SunStar)

A few days ago, I received an interesting – and intriguing – information from one of my sources in Manila. He said, *"How can you crush the ASG (Abu Sayyaf aka Abu Shabu) when it's an open secret that the Chinese financier of these bandits is close to so many powerful people? He's believed to instigate the Mautes to create a situation in Marawi to divert the attention of the AFP who are almost done in apprehending all of them to put closure to ASG. This Chinese who uses his being a converted Muslim to lord it over basically owning all big businesses Sulu and Mindanao wide, wants to protect his puppet Hapilon by floating the disinfo that he escaped the military cordon in Marawi.*

"If the concerned people of Marawi is serious in finishing this tragedy, they should act asap like the Boholanos helping the PNP and AFP in getting all the remnants of ASG. Huwag na tayo maglokohan, kawawa mga sundalo at peaceful Muslims na nadadamay sa kalokohan

ng iilan na may hidden agenda. Sobra na. (Let's not fool with ourselves. It's a pity the soldiers and peaceful Muslims are dragged into this foolishness of a few people with hidden agenda. It's too much)."

Link to drug lords

During a recent media briefing, PNP Chief Ronald "Bato" dela Rosa confirmed the Maute group's link to drug lords. He said that the Maute group is known to have "protected" the drug lords as early as last year.

My source also said that some of these militants have business relationships with some government officials, which makes one wonder: Are the Maute militants working as mercenaries for those behind the Marawi attack and are paid through the "matriarch"?

During a recent media briefing, PNP Chief Ronald "Bato" dela Rosa confirmed the Maute group's link to drug lords. He said that the Maute group is known to have "protected" the drug lords as early as last year. He said that he received information that majority of the drug lords in Metro Manila, Luzon and Visayas went to Marawi City a year ago to hold a "drug summit." He added that the drug lords were protected by the Maute group and narco-politicians. Surmise it to say, Marawi appears to be the "Vatican" of the illegal drug cartel in the country.

Underground fortifications

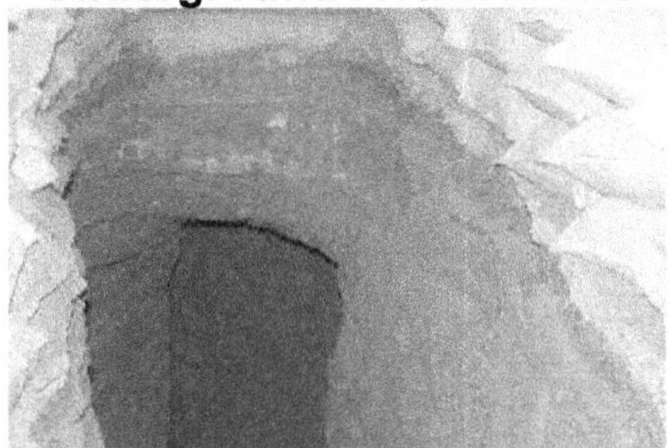

One of the Maute group's underground bunker/tunnels discovered by the Philippine forces when they breached the Maute's defensive positions in Marawi.

When the government forces breached the Maute's defensive positions, they discovered bombproof tunnels used by the militants as bunker and bomb shelters. The military spokesman said that the roughly 10 percent of Marawi held by the Maute militants has many tunnels and basements that can withstand 500-pound bombs.

Clearly, the underground fortifications couldn't have been built in the short time since the "Marawi attack" commenced last May 23. They must already have been constructed long before that date, which is to suggest that the Maute's presence in Marawi may have been a common knowledge to the city residents. The question is: Is the military aware of their presence long before the siege? I believe so. But for as long as the Maute group stays out of "trouble," the military would stay out of their way. It was a *de facto* coexistence between the Maute group and government forces.

But on May 23, the military decided to arrest Isnilon Hapilon, who was believed to be in Marawi City. Hapilon is on the FBI's "most wanted terrorists list" with a $5 million bounty offered for his capture, which was a good enough reason to arrest him. It was then that the Maute group purportedly "entered" Marawi and clashed with government troops.

Armed President Duterte was all set to visit the troops in Marawi City on July 7 but bad weather stood in the way. (MALACAÑANG)

The botched attempt to arrest Hapilon led to open warfare between government forces and the Maute group. With Hapilon out of sight — either dead or out of the country — and the Maute group leaderless and in disarray, it's just a matter of time for the fighting to come to an end. But it would a devastated city and grieving people that would suffer for a long time from the atrocity of the "Marawi attack."

ooooo

4
The Folly of Federalism Redux

July 10, 2017

Apolinario Mabini and Gen. Emilio Aguinaldo.

President Rodrigo Duterte's top legislative agenda is the federalism of the Philippines. Actually, federalism was not the idea of Duterte, two of our national heroes, Emilio Aguinaldo and Apolinario Mabini, were the first to suggest dividing the Philippine Islands into three federal states: Luzon, Visayas, and Mindanao.

More than a half century later, former president of the University of the Philippines Dr. Jose Abueva proposed and argued that a federal form of government was necessary to more efficiently cater to the needs of the country despite its diversity. He said that the primary goals of a constitutional amendment is to increase decentralization, greater local power and access to resources most especially among regions outside Metro Manila which has long been dubbed as rather imperial. Aside from Abueva, senator Aquilino Pimentel Jr. was a prominent supporter of federalism who had advocated federalism since 2001. He saw the proposed system as a key component in alleviating the Mindanao crisis and appeasing Moro insurgents. He argued that federalism will also hasten economic development since resource and financial mobilization is upon each states' or provinces' discretion without significant constraint from the central government. [Source: Wikipedia]

During the presidential elections of 2004, president Gloria Macapagal Arroyo campaigned for constitutional reforms. After winning the elections, she created the Consultative Commission, headed by Dr. Abueva. The task of the commission was "to propose the necessary revisions on the 1987 Constitution that included a shift to a unicameral parliamentary form of government, decentralization of national government, and empowering local governments by a transition to a parliamentary-federal government system."

Rally against Pres. Gloria Macapagal Arroyo's Charter Change movement in 2004.

The proponents of charter change, while agreeing on a parliamentary system, are divided between the supporters of Federalism and those that decry Federalism as an unworkable political system. Instead, the anti-federalist group is pushing for the adoption of a unitary parliamentary system.

President Rodrigo Duterte campaigns for federalism.

Today, President Duterte is pushing hard to change the government to a federal system using the model similar to the one proposed by Abueva in 2004. He has been pressuring the House of Representatives to pass legislation to effect a charter change. Well, it doesn't seem as easy as it sounds.

While a unitary government – the central government — has all the power, federalism would seem to be more democratic. But don't be fooled by it. There are lots of variables and unknowns before the House could responsibly fashion the necessary amendments to fit the fundamental tenets of a Philippine democratic system as enshrined in the 1987 Constitution.

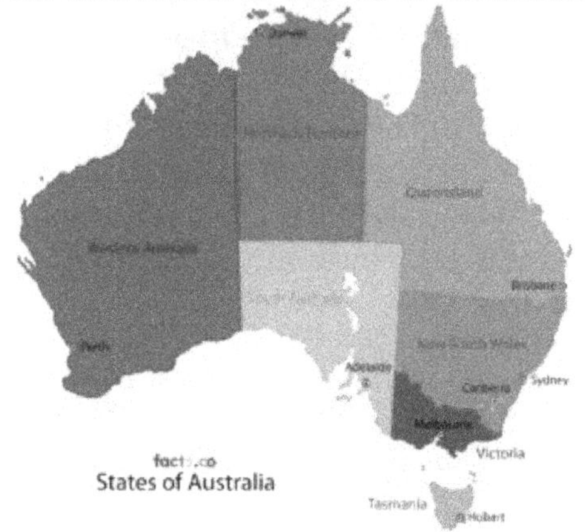

Australia divided into six states.

Allow me to share excerpt from my column, *"The Folly of Federalism,"* which I wrote in October 2005. I said, *"To get a pretty good 'feel' of how Federalism works, let's look at Australia. In 1901, Australia adopted the Federal Parliament and government with the six States giving up some of their powers, but remaining independent. The Australian Constitution states, 'The legislative power of the commonwealth shall be vested in a Federal Parliament.' In addition, the constitution gives a range of powers and responsibilities to the Federal Parliament.*

Powers not identified in the constitution reside with the States. Each of the six States has its own constitution, parliament and government.

"But there is a lot of overlapping between the Australian Federal and the State governments. A history of competition between the Federal government and the State governments exists. Since the Federal government controls tax collection, it has established its dominance in the political system. The States became dependent on Federal financial assistance. [www.AustralianPolitics.com]

"In terms of tax collections, the website says, the Federal government gets 70-80% of all tax revenues. The Federal government then divides the expenditure of the tax revenues between the Federal and State governments. This created ongoing financial negotiations — and haggling — between the Federal government and the States.

"There are advantages and disadvantages of Australian Federalism. However, the disadvantages far outweigh the advantages, some of which are: duplication of government; overlapping or conflicting policies in different parts of the country; State education systems with differing curricula and grading methods; financial inequality which leads to unhealthy competition and rivalry between the States; neglect in important areas of, to cite a few, public policy and public transportation; and over-government. The website claims, 'It is often argued that a nation of 19 million people cannot afford to have 15 houses of parliament, plus hundreds of local governments.'

"According to a study conducted by the University of Sydney, the question was asked: 'Has Federalism outlived its usefulness in Australia?' The study concluded: 'It is obvious that the advantages no longer exist and the advantages are overweighed by the numerous disadvantages. It is truly time for Australia to make major reforms for it to remain an effective government process.' "

Federalism for the Philippines

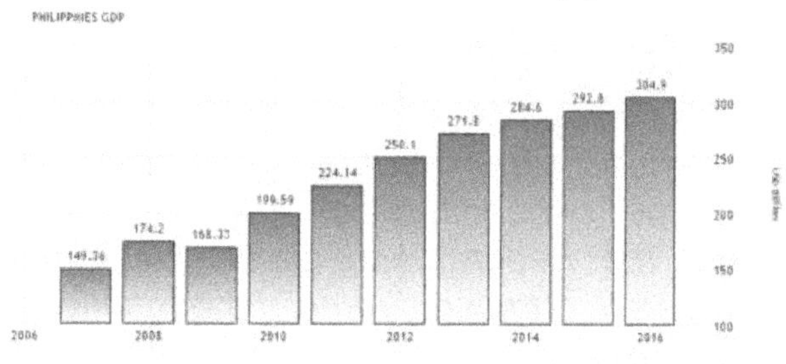

Philippines' GDP from 2007-2016.

Given the advantages and disadvantages of Australian-style Federalism, it begs the question: Should the Philippines pursue a Federal system of government?

In my opinion, Federalism for the Philippines is a folly. Let's look at some numbers. Its Gross Domestic Product (GDP) was worth $304.9 billion in 2016 and the GDP per capita was $7,728 (ranked 118 by International Monetary Fund) compared to Australia's $48,899 (ranked 17). Simply put, the Philippines would not be able to afford the cost of Federalism.

First of all, most of the big industries and manpower resources are concentrated in Metro

Manila and its surrounding provinces, Cebu City, Davao City and a few other places. Provinces that are agricultural-based would be hard-pressed to collect taxes to maintain their government structure, which would consist of a legislative body, judicial system, education system, health professionals, law enforcement, social services and several other agencies. After the Federal government has taken its bigger share of the tax revenues, the amount left for the regional governments would not be enough to sustain their existence.

ARMM and CAR

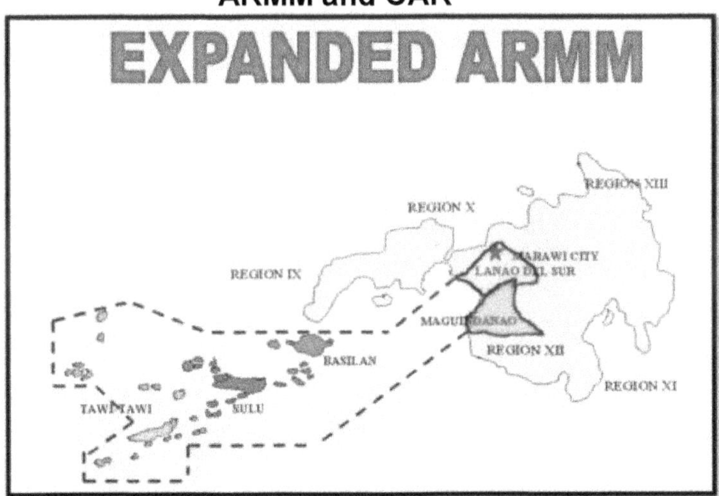

Map of the expanded area of ARMM.

In 1989, the law creating the Autonomous Region in Muslim Mindanao (ARMM) was passed. It was composed of the provinces of Basilan, Lanao del Sur, Maguindanao, Sulu, and Tawi-Tawi and the cities of Marawi and Lamitan.

The political intent was to satisfy the aspirations of the Bangsamoro people for self-rule and self-determination. It was created to address the "Moro problem." But instead of solving the "Moro problem," ARMM divided Bangsamoro into several factions run by regional warlords.

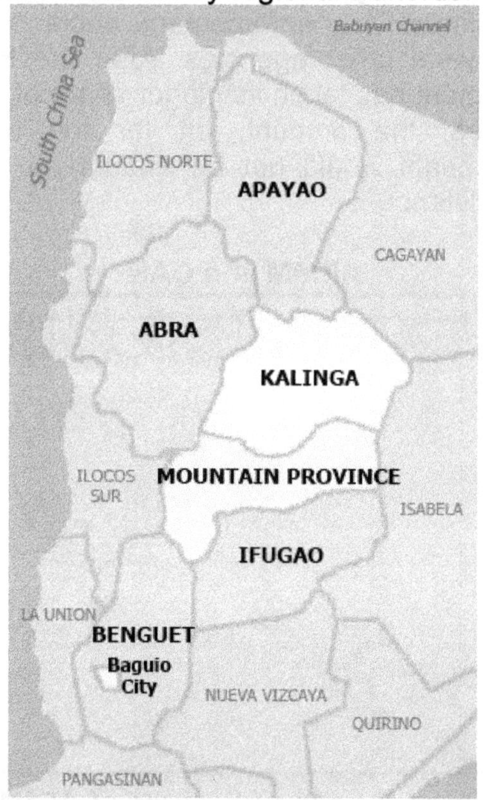

Map of Cordillera Autonomous Region.

In 1997, the Philippines passed Republic Act 8438 creating the Cordillera Autonomous Region (CAR), which states: *"The Cordillera Autonomous Region is a territorial and political subdivision administered by the Regional*

Autonomous Government consisting of the regional government and local government units under the general supervision of the President of the Republic of the Philippines." However, it failed to pass the approval of the Cordillera peoples in a region-wide referendum in 1998. Today, CAR exists as Cordillera Administrative Region.

On paper, ARMM and CAR are ideally suited to address the "needs" of the Bangsamoro people and the cultural minorities in the Cordillera region, comprised Abra, Apayao, Benguet, Ifugao, Kalinga, and Mountain Province. However, ARMM and CAR do not have the financial independence or the ability to create revenue-generating industry. As a result they become pauper entities that depend on the central government for all the things they need to function as "autonomous" regions.

Some people argue that a Federal government is the only way to give freedom and independence to the Filipinos. In today's globalized economy, what is freedom and independence? In my opinion, freedom is "financial freedom" and independence is "financial independence." Real freedom and real independence can only be achieved with wealth and the ability to compete in the global market. If we free the Filipinos into creating their own country without financial freedom, then they will become slaves of their own country.

ooooo

5
"Martial Law Kuno"
June 23, 2017

Philippine Marines patrol Marawi City.

Long before President Rodrigo "Digong" Duterte imposed martial law in Mindanao, he was already toying with the idea of declaring martial law, not just in Mindanao but the entire country. Why? What caused him to consider martial law when his supporters in the House of Representatives have provided him with an ironclad defense from any attempt to impeach him? Or are there other reasons – secret and unpublished – that would satisfy his private agenda?

For one thing, one can say that Duterte was a democratically elected "strongman" like Russian President Vladimir Putin. While Duterte is not a "dictator" in the mold of the late President Ferdinand E. Marcos, he was able to exercise near-absolute power in pushing his legislative agenda. Indeed, senators and congressmen who opposed his wishes were severely dealt with.

In the House of Representatives, except for a few party-list congressmen, nobody dares oppose his legislative agenda that includes restoration of the death penalty, the switch to a federal government, and lowering of the age of criminal liability. The House Speaker, Rep. Pantaleon Alvarez, a protégée of Duterte, is totally supportive of his legislative agenda. And the congressmen – who are *balimbings* (political turncoats) as a matter of political survival – fear him.

In my column, ***"Is martial law just a matter of time?"*** *(January 27, 2017),* I asked: *"Why would Digong [Duterte] want to declare martial law, when his grip to power is strong? Would it be fair to presume that he might have been thinking of the day when his grip weakens and loses control of Congress? And the specter of that happening could give him sleepless nights, insecurity, and paranoia. Could this be the reason why he is not comfortable sleeping in Malacañang Palace protected by the elite Presidential Security Group?"*

Narco list

President Rodrigo Duterte announces the *"narco list."*

When the Philippine National Police (PNP) submitted an intelligence report – "Narco list" – to Duterte, several judges' names were included on the report. Duterte threatened to have them arrested. Supreme Court Chief Justice Ma. Lourdes Sereno strongly opposed it and issued a statement that said, *"Law enforcers must first secure warrants of arrest from judges before judges allow themselves to be 'physically accountable to any police officer' as she warned of a constitutional crisis."* This did not bode well with Duterte who responded angrily, *"I'm giving you a warning. Don't create a crisis because I will order everybody in the executive department not to honor you,"* he said referring to Sereno. He added, *"Please, don't order me. I'm not a fool. If this continues, [that] you're tying to stop me, I might lose my cool. Or would you rather I declare martial law?"* But Duterte relented and the matter with the "narco judges" was dropped.

Battle of Marawi

Battle of Marawi. Philippine Marines attack Maute stronghold.

On May 23, 2017 while Duterte was enroute to Moscow for a five-day visit, the rebel group Maute struck. At about 2:00 PM, the Battle of Marawi began. At least 500 members of Maute attacked a Philippine Army brigade stationed at Camp Ranao in Marawi City. They were seen rampaging through the streets waving ISIS black flags.

While in Moscow, Duterte declared martial law at 10:00 pm that same day. He cut short his visit after meeting Russian President Vladimir Putin for a short time. In an attempt to acquire weapons from Russia, Putin told him to provide a "shopping list" and he'd look at it. Duterte flew back home without the "bacon" he had expected to bring home.

Philippine Marine Commandant Major General Emmanuel Salamat (R) listens to US military representatives during a handover ceremony of weapons from the US military, at the Marine headquarters in Manila on June 5, 2017. Photo by Ted Aljibe/AFP

Last June 5, the U.S. handed over – I mean, given free — $150 million worth of brand-new weapons that included 300 M4 assault rifles, 100 grenade launchers, and four M134D Gatling-style machine guns that can fire thousands of rounds a minute. The U.S. Embassy issued a statement, saying: *"This equipment will enhance the [Philippine Marines'] counterterrorism capabilities, and help protect [troops] actively engaged in counterterrorism operations in the southern Philippines."*

It's interesting to note that on June 2 — a few days before the handover – Duterte had complained about the quality of "secondhand" American military hardware. *"I will not accept any more military equipment that is secondhand. The ones the Americans are giving, I do not want that anymore,"* he said.

Boots on the ground

Joint Training: US soldiers train a member of the Philippine Coast Guard during one of their joint exercises in Mindanao. (Photo from Joint Special Operations Task Force-Philippines)

But weapons were not the only ones Uncle Sam had given free. A Pentagon spokesman, U.S. Navy Cmdr. Gary Ross, confirmed the presence of 50 to 100 special-operations forces that are helping the Philippine marines in Marawi. He said that the U.S. also maintains a force of 300 to 500 to support regular bilateral training, exercises, and other activities in the country. He said that they're in Marawi to provide technical assistance to the Philippine troops. However, they're authorized to fire back if attacked.

In addition, another U.S. official, speaking on condition of anonymity, said that the support included aerial surveillance and targeting, electronic eavesdropping, communications assistance, and training.

One might question the presence of U.S. troops in the country, which the Philippine Constitution bans. Philippine military spokesman Brig. Gen. Restituto Padilla told reporters in Manila, *"The presence of armed U.S. troops in Marawi was covered by a 1951 Mutual Defense Treaty, which calls for both parties to aid each other in times of enemy aggression."* He added, *"That capacity has been moved to help ground forces in Marawi, and that arrangement should not complicate our military engagement."*

Who's in charge?

President Rodrigo Duterte and his generals.

But what is strange is that the day after the handover of U.S. weapons, Duterte held a press conference and told the reporters that he "never approached America" for help. He said that he was "entirely unaware of their presence until they [the Americans] arrived." But while he claimed that he didn't ask for U.S. military help, it begs the question: Did the Philippine military request the aid independently without consulting Duterte? To avoid embarrassment, Duterte told the media that might have been the case. He said that due to years of U.S. training, "our soldiers are pro-American, that I cannot deny." However, he did not comment on whether the Philippine military asked for U.S. help without his "approval." And this raises the question: Who is in charge?

Martial law chain of command: AFP Chief Gen. Eduardo Año as the chief martial law implementor (L); Defense Secretary Delfin Lorenzana, a retired major general, as martial law administrator in Mindanao (Center); and President Rodrigo Duterte (R).

While one may wonder whether Duterte is still in charge, the answer is Yes and No. Yes, because he is still the president of the Philippines. No, because by declaring martial law, he turned over certain government functions to the military. He designated Defense Secretary Delfin Lorenzana, a retired major general, as martial law administrator in Mindanao and Armed forces of the Philippines (AFP) Chief Gen. Eduardo Año as the chief martial law implementor. Año will be directly under the deputy martial administrator, who has yet to be named. He will also work with PNP Director General Ronald dela Rosa.

Indeed, little did Duterte realize that he had more power before de declared martial law. With martial law, he has to carefully work with the generals, giving them a lot of latitude. And to make sure that they remain loyal, he has to share power with them. Indeed, they can make or break him. And he knows that.

The late dictator Ferdinand E. Marcos and son, former Sen. Ferdinand (Bongbong) Marcos Jr.

So, are you for or against martial law? As the Visayans would say it, "Martial law *kuno*," while the Tagalogs would say, "Martial law *daw*." But the Ilocanos will always say, "Marcos *pa rin kami!*" And Bongbong Marcos would be so delighted and he would say, "Martial law forever!" But the powerless and poor common tao could only say, "*Hay naku,* here we go again!" And for Donald Trump, he can only say, "It's fake news." And guess what Digong would be saying? "Sons of whores!"

Ooooo

6
Vietnam: Uncle Sam's Newest Ally?

June 14, 2017

South Vietnamese general shoots suspected Viet Cong official in the head. (Ed Adams/AP).

Once enemies, the U.S. and Vietnam have become friends over the course of four decades.

While it did not happen overnight, what transpired was a slow process of rapprochement between the two countries. It took two generations of Vietnamese and Americans to set aside the bitterness they both have on each other. Why not?

More than 58,000 American and 282,000 South Vietnamese soldiers were killed from 1955 to 1975. North Vietnam and the Viet Cong suffered 444,000 military casualties and 627,000 civilian deaths.

Last day of Vietnam War: South Vietnamese fleeing from the North Vietnamese try to get into a U.S. Marine helicopter on top of a tower at the U.S. Embassy in Saigon.

After the fall of Saigon, tens of thousands of South Vietnamese civilians and former soldiers fled the country. Known as "boat people," the refugees used boats of all sizes to escape the North Vietnamese communists. They migrated to other countries, in particular the nearby Philippines where the government resettled them. However, the U.S. was their country of choice; thus, the process of looking for sponsors began. American families opened their homes and welcomed them. Eventually, most of them were able to find jobs and own their homes. Over time, the Vietnamese immigrants were allowed to petition for family members provided that they have jobs and financial capability to put them up. By 2014, 1.3 million Vietnamese immigrants resided in the U.S.

Beyond the strong affinity displayed by the Vietnamese people toward their former enemies, government-to-government relations between the U.S. and Vietnam improved considerably. Cultural and economic ties progressed at a pace that surpassed the most optimistic expectations.

Obama and Vietnam

President Barack Obama and his Vietnamese counterpart Truong Tan Sang shake hands at their meeting in Washington, DC.

On July 25, 2013, the historic meeting between President Barack Obama and his Vietnamese counterpart Truong Tan Sang in Washington, DC broke new ground in U.S.-

Vietnam bilateral relations. Obama and Truong decided to form a U.S.-Vietnam Comprehensive Partnership, which underlined the principles of *"respect for the U.N. Charter, international law, and each other's political systems, independence, sovereignty, and territorial integrity."* The two leaders pledged that their countries would continue to cooperate on defense and security matters.

On May 23, 2016, Obama visited Hanoi and announced that the U.S. would fully lift a longstanding embargo on lethal arms sale to Vietnam, a decision that may have been precipitated by China's military build-up in the South China Sea (SCS). Obama said that the lifting of the arms embargo *"will ensure Vietnam has access to the equipment it needs to defend itself and removes a lingering vestige of the Cold War."*

Trump and Vietnam

President Donald Trump and Vietnamese Prime Minister Nguyen Xuan Phuc shake hands at their meeting in Washington, DC.

Recently, Vietnamese Prime Minister Nguyen Xuan Phuc visited President Donald J. Trump in the White House. His visit is significant because there have been perceptions that Vietnam was leaning to China, and the U.S. is veering away from the Indo-Asia-Pacific region. This caused many countries in the region – including Vietnam and the Philippines – to move closer to China. The leaders of the other eight ASEAN countries are adjusting their alignment as well. They're preparing themselves in the event that Trump would leave the region altogether.

But the U.S. visit of Nguyen has changed all that. Nguyen was the first ASEAN leader to visit Washington, DC since Trump was inaugurated president. With the meeting of Trump and Nguyen in the White House on May 31, it was evident that Trump is not reversing the course of U.S. policy in the Indo-Asia-Pacific region. The "Pivot to Asia" that Obama started may have changed in name, but the objectives are the same: to protect U.S. interests in the Indo-Asia-Pacific region.

The meeting between the two leaders produced a joint statement to "Enhance the Comprehensive Partnership between the U.S. and Vietnam." Their joint statement reiterates that the *"United States is a 'Pacific power with widespread interests and commitments throughout the Asia Pacific.' It maintains all elements of the U.S.-Vietnam Comprehensive Partnership that was established during the Obama administration. It goes a step further, stating that President Trump and Prime Minister [Nguyen] Phuc are committed to making the partnership 'deeper, more substantive, and more effective.' For the first time the two former enemies stress at the summit level their 'pledge to strengthen cooperation in the fields of security and intelligence.' "*

Which makes one wonder: Is this just another diplomatic hyperbole or does it seem like it would lead to stronger defense and economic ties between the two countries? While a defense treaty would not be politically feasible at this time as it would certainly irk China and would also affect Vietnamese-Russian security relations, an arrangement similar to the U.S.-India Logistics Exchange Memorandum of Agreement (LEMOA) just might do the work. But while LEMOA might fall short of a "basing agreement," it gives the militaries of both countries access to each other's facilities for supplies and repair. It's a good start that could lead to a *de facto* – if not official – defense arrangement.

With this new U.S.-Vietnam Enhanced Comprehensive Partnership, the two countries would be able to deter China's aggressive behavior in the SCS; thus, protect Vietnam's EEZ from Chinese encroachment. Indeed, what is at stake is Vietnam's economic interest in the SCS.

Defense cooperation and the SCS issue were prominently addressed in the joint statement. Trump and Nguyen affirmed that the SCS is a "waterway of strategic significance." They also discussed the possibility of a visit to a Vietnamese port – Cam Ranh Bay — by a U.S. aircraft carrier and steps to further cooperation between their two naval forces.

Vietnam will never forget the Battle of the Paracel Islands in 1974 when China occupied the islands, which are claimed by Vietnam. Vietnam attempted to expel the Chinese Navy from the vicinity. A battle ensued and the Chinese forces prevailed. China established *de facto* control over the Paracels. However, Vietnam maintained her claim over the Paracels to this day.

A "first" in U.S.-Vietnam relations

China deploys giant oil rig in the waters near the Paracel Islands.

In 2014, China deployed her biggest oil rig into Vietnam's exclusive economic zone (EEZ). Vietnam then sent to the U.S. her number two man on the ruling Politburo, Executive Secretary of the Communist Party of Vietnam Dinh The Huynh. That was a "first" in U.S.-Vietnam relations.

Indeed, for the most part of the last two decades, the Philippines and Singapore led the rest of ASEAN in engaging the U.S. With the rift that Philippine President Rodrigo Duterte has with the U.S., the Philippines has cocooned herself into isolation. With the vacuum created by the Philippines, Vietnam would be more than willing to play a key role in engagement with the U.S.

U.S. donates six coastal patrol boats to Vietnam.

As a sign of closer U.S.-Vietnam military ties, the U.S. transferred six patrol boats to the Vietnam Coast Guard last May. The U.S. embassy released a statement, which said, *"The handover represented deepening cooperation to maritime law enforcement and humanitarian assistance in Vietnam's territorial waters and exclusive economic zone."*

U.S. Secretary of Defense James Mattis (5th L) poses for a picture with ASEAN defense leaders after a meeting on the sidelines of the 16th IISS Shangri-La Dialogue in Singapore, June 4, 2017.

At the recently concluded Shangri-La Dialogue in Singapore, U.S. Defense Secretary James Mattis said during his address to some 500 delegates: *"The US can't accept Chinese actions that impinge on the interests of the international community, undermining the rules-based order that has benefited all countries represented here today including, and especially, China."* He added that while conflict with China is not "inevitable," the two countries will engage in competition. And that's where Uncle Sam needs reliable allies to compete with China, which begs the question: Is Vietnam emerging as Uncle Sam's newest ally in the Indo-Asia-Pacific region?

ooooo

7
Trump's Geopolitical Miscalculations

May 12, 2017

U.S. President Donald J. Trump.

When Donald J. Trump was campaigning for the presidency, he projected a "tough guy" image by lambasting everyone that stood on his way or anyone who disagreed with him. His forays into foreign policy were gutsy and digressed from previous administrations' diplomatic restraint in handling sensitive geopolitical issues. He shocked America's NATO allies after he suggested that he might not honor the core tenet of the military alliance. He said the U.S. "would not necessarily defend new NATO members in the Baltics in the event of Russian attack if he were elected to the White House."

On U.S.-China relations, Trump stirred a hornet's nest when he challenged the "One-China Policy" and accused China of currency manipulation and unfair trade practices. He vowed to straighten things out in Asia.

His tough stance against China gave Japan and South Korea, America's closest treaty allies, a sigh of relief. At last, they have an American president who would stand by them if attacked, unlike Trump's predecessor, former president Barack Obama, whom he criticized for appeasing China and didn't do anything to stop China's construction of artificial islands in the Spratly archipelago.

After he assumed the presidency, he must have realized that foreign policy – which he had no experience before – is a complicated and complex game of statesmanship and adroit diplomatic leadership and maneuvering. It must have been a rude awakening for him to recognize that the practice of brinkmanship is quite different from the "art of the deal," which he proudly claims to be his forte.

And to make things worse, he appointed his friend Rex Tillerson to the post of Secretary of State. With no experience in foreign policy – or government for that matter – poor Tillerson was thrown into the murky waters of geopolitics. And between him and Trump, how do you think they'd handle bullies like Vladimir Putin, Xi Jinping, and Kim Jong-un in the world stage? They are no ordinary world leaders; they are authoritarian dictators who love to threaten the U.S. with nuclear destruction. In particular, North Korea's "Supreme Leader" Kim Jong-un seems to have rankled Trump who doesn't appear to know how to handle the unpredictable Kim.

North Korea problem

U.S. Vice President Mike Pence at the DMZ.

In an attempt to show Kim that he meant business, Trump sent Vice President Mike Pence to South Korea. In a show of grit, Pence — like Trump and Tillerson who don't have any foreign policy experience — visited the demilitarized zone (DMZ) and stared across the "no man's land" between North and South Korea, a day after North Korea's failed missile launch. He talked tough, saying, "There was a period of strategic patience [in reference to Obama's foreign policy] but the era of strategic patience is over." "All options are on the table to achieve the objectives and ensure the stability of the people of this country," he told reporters while propaganda music was continually played across from the North Korean side.

Meanwhile, Trump announced that an "armada" consisting of an aircraft carrier and several warships were on their way to the Korean Peninsula as a warning to North Korea. But a few days later, it was revealed in the media that the "armada" was moving in the opposite direction: to Australia to participate in a training exercise. In a quick attempt to undo his boo-boo, Trump ordered the "armada" to turn around and head to the Korean Peninsula.

USS Carl Vinson battle group.

But while the exercise of sending the blunt-talking vice president and deploying the "armada" to Korean waters may have achieved a "shock and awe" effect initially, it was blown away by Trump's erroneous announcement.

What happened with the "armada" may have been deemed as miscommunication between Trump and his admirals. But from a geopolitical standpoint, Trump lost credibility as

Commander-in-Chief, which effectively dealt a major blow to his ability to lead the nation's military. For not getting his ducks in a row, Trump's miscalculation doesn't bode well with his relation with Asian countries, particularly the 10 members of the Association of Southeast Asian Nations (ASEAN). Most of the ASEAN members are now kowtowing to Beijing because of their perception that Trump has abandoned Obama's "Pivot to Asia" policy that has kept most of them in America's orbit.

South China Sea concessions

Ivanka Trump and her Chinese trademark.

After the recent Trump-Xi summit at Mar-a-Lago in Florida, Trump's hard-line stance against China melted like a marshmallow over a fire. After two days of negotiations, Trump declared that China was not a "currency manipulator" and decided to maintain the status quo on trade issues.

For these concessions, Trump wanted Xi to help with the North Korea problem. In return, Xi responded with his signature half-smile but made no promises. But if there was one winner during the summit, it was Trump's daughter Ivanka Trump whose three trademarks for her jewelry and spa brand were approved by China the same day she and her husband Jared Kushner sat down for dinner with Xi and Trump at the Mar-a-Lago. It's interesting to note that the Chinese trademarks requires that Ivanka's products be manufactured in China using Chinese workers, which begs the question: What happened to Trump's "America First" slogan? Or is it still the same old "Made in China" trade policies? Does it sound like another miscalculation? Indeed, the calculus doesn't add up in America's favor. Two winners emerged from the summit: Xi Jinping and Ivanka Trump.

TPP miscalculation

Trans-Pacific Partnership.

But the worst in Trump's miscalculations in Asia was his decision to pull out of the Trans-Pacific Partnership (TPP), a security and economic agreement between 12 countries led by the U.S. Seven of the member-countries hail from the Asia-Pacific: Australia, Brunei, Japan, Malaysia, New Zealand, Singapore, and Vietnam, of which four are ASEAN members (Brunei, Malaysia, Singapore, and Vietnam). Collectively, the TPP member-countries account for 40% of world trade. Ironically, it was the U.S. under the presidency of Obama who started the negotiations among the 12 countries. Unfortunately, while 11 countries ratified TPP in 2016, the U.S. Congress under Republican control failed – or refused – to ratify it in the last few months of Obama's presidency. When Trump took over, withdrawal from TPP was one of his first acts – victims of his vindictive assault on policies and programs that Obama implemented.

Following Trump's withdrawal last February, Japan (the largest remaining TPP member) said that the TPP was meaningless without the U.S. But recently, Japan's position on TPP changed. She realized that China is moving fast to fill the vacuum left by the U.S. in the Pacific Rim region. And without the U.S. the other member-countries are playing the "China card" by negotiating their own trade agreements with China. Among them are Canada and Mexico, two of the three member-countries of the North American Free Trade Agreement (NAFTA). The third member-country is the U.S. But what made Canada and Mexico nervous was Trump's threat to withdraw from NAFTA. But it was averted when the Canadian prime minister and Mexican president called Trump and talked him out of withdrawing. Needless to say, it would have been another humongous miscalculation had Trump decided to dismantle NAFTA.

Japan steps in

Japanese Prime Minister Shinzo Abe.

It finally dawned on Japanese Prime Minister Shinzo Abe that if China joins the TPP, she would end up controlling the partnership, which would make Abe play second fiddle to China. And given the current geopolitical tremors that are occurring between Japan and China over the disputed Senkaku Islands in the East China Sea, Japan is considering taking over the reins of the TPP.

Trump withdrawing from TPP.

With all of Trump's geopolitical miscalculations, he could lose America's preeminent role in world affairs. While Pax Americana has been showing cracks on it façade, the U.S. under Obama managed to contain

China. But just four months into Trump's presidency, China's takeover of South China Sea is secured. With Trump making all these miscalculations, Pax Americana is on the throes of death. And taking its place would be a bipolar world order: Pax Russica in the West and Pax Sinica in the East.

Ooooo

8
The ICC Case Against Duterte
May 1, 2017

President Rodrigo Duterte and the International Criminal Court.

On November 17, 2016, President Rodrigo Duterte, before heading to Lima, Peru, told the media he just might order the Philippines' withdrawal from the International Criminal Court (ICC). He got the idea following Russian President Vladimir Putin's withdrawal of Russia's membership from ICC, who the day before had signed an order to formally withdraw Russia's signature from the founding statute of the ICC. He claimed that ICC was "one-sided and inefficient" and that the ICC had failed to live up to "hopes of the international community."

Russia signed the Rome Statute in 2000 that set up the ICC, the world's first permanent court that investigates genocide, war crimes, and crimes against humanity. Russia said she was unhappy with the ICC's treatment of the case on Russia's short war with Georgia in 2008, saying the ICC ignored the aggression of Georgia against civilians in South Ossetia – a pro-Russia separatist region of Georgia. But the truth of the matter is it was Russia who invaded Georgia in support of South Ossetia's secession from Georgia. Many believed that Putin's withdrawal was triggered by ICC's published report that classified the Russian annexation of Crimea as an "occupation."

Other countries that had served notice to withdraw from the ICC are Gambia, South Africa, and Burundi, who had charged that the ICC had been used "for the persecution of Africans and especially their leaders, while ignoring crimes committed by the West."

To date, the ICC has opened investigations into 10 situations in: (1) the Democratic Republic of the Congo; (2) Uganda; (3) the Central African Republic I; (4) Darfur, Sudan; (5) Kenya; (6) Libya; the (7) Côte d'Ivoire; (8) Mali; (9) the Central African Republic II; and (10) Georgia. The ICC has publicly indicted 40 people. It has issued arrest warrants for 32 individuals and summonses to eight others.

Seven persons are in detention. Proceedings against 23 are ongoing: 10 are at large as fugitives, four are under arrest but not in the Court's custody, eight are at trial, and one is appealing his conviction. Proceedings against 17 have been completed: three have been convicted, one has been acquitted, six have had the charges against them dismissed, two have had the charges against them withdrawn, one has had his case declared inadmissible, and four have died before trial. *[Source: Wikipedia]*

Among them was the late dictator Muammar Gaddafi and his son Saif al-Islam Gaddafi, who were both killed in the aftermath of the Libyan revolution.

So far, four had been convicted, to wit:

Jean-Pierre Bemba Gombo –
A politician in the Democratic Republic of the Congo. He leads the Movement for the Liberation of the Congo (MLC), a rebel group turned political party. He was elected president in 2006 and senator in 2007. On May 24, 2008, he was arrested near Brussels on the basis of an arrest warrant issued by the ICC. He was charged with two counts of crimes against humanity and

three counts of war crimes. On March 21, 2016, he was convicted on these charges. On June 21, 2016, he was imprisoned on a 19-year sentence following a landmark conviction at the ICC. In September 2016, he appealed against his conviction alleging a mistrial. He awaits further sentencing for corruptly influencing witnesses through means of bribery during his trial for war crimes.

Germain Katanga (aka Simba) –
A former leader of the Patriotic Resistance Force in Ituri (FRPI) in the Democratic Republic of the Congo. On October17, 2007, the Congolese authorities surrendered him to the ICC to stand trial on six counts of war crimes and three counts of crimes against humanity. The charges include murder, sexual slavery, rape, willful killing, and directing crimes against civilians, to name a few. On March 7, 2014, the ICC convicted Katanga on five counts of war crimes and crimes against humanity as an accessory to the February 2003 massacre in the village of Bogoro. The verdict was the second-ever conviction in the 12 years of operation of the ICC. It followed the 2012 conviction of Thomas Lubanga Dyilo.

Thomas Lubanga Dyilo –
A convicted war criminal from the Democratic Republic of the Congo, he was the first person ever convicted by the ICC. He led the Union of Congolese Patriots (UPC) and was a key player in the Ituri conflict. On March 17,2006, her became the fist person arrested under a warrant issued by the ICC. He was charged of "conscripting and enlisting children under the age of 15 and using them to participate actively in hostilities." On July 10, 2012, he was found guilty and sentenced to 14 years of imprisonment.

Ahmad al-Faqi al-Mahdi (aka Abu Tourab) – He was a member of Ansar Dine, a Tuareg Islamist militia in North Africa. In 2006, he pleaded guilty in the ICC for the war crime of attacking religious and historical buildings in the Malian city of Timbuktu. He was the first person convicted by the ICC for such a crime. He was sentenced to nine years in prison.

Complaint against Duterte

Sen. Leila de Lima.

Last October, Sen. Leila de Lima called for an international investigation into the country's drug war, which had left 4,000 people dead during Duterte 's first four months in office. De Lima, a former justice secretary said that the extrajudicial killings (EJKs) must end and that the ICC should investigate them.

The following month, Duterte came to the attention of the ICC. An ICC judge said she was closely monitoring Duterte's "war on drugs" for possible human rights violations.

Attorney Jude Sabio in front of the ICC building.

Last April 24, attorney Jude Sabio, a lawyer for confessed hitman Edgar Matobato, filed a 77-page criminal complaint against Duterte and at least 11 senior government officials in the International Criminal Court (ICC) in The Hague, the Netherlands. The complaint alleges that Duterte and the others were liable for murder and called for an investigation, arrest warrants, and a trial. Sabio said that Duterte "repeatedly, unchangingly and continuously" committed crimes against humanity and that under him, killing drug suspects and other criminals has become "best practice."

Hitman Edgar Matobato testifies before a Senate panel.

The complaint was based on the testimony of Matobato and another confessed hitman, retired policeman Arturo Lascanas, and statements from rights groups and media reports, including a recent Reuters series detailing the killings. The question is: What are the chances of convicting Duterte based on Sabio's complaint? It's not easy. And the fact that Duterte would still be president until May 2022, it would be very unlikely to bring him to trial.

The ICC'ing of Duterte

"Stop Summary Killings" rally in Manila.

Since 2002, the ICC has received over 12,000 complaints or communications, of which nine have gone to trial and six verdicts have been delivered. The ICC has no powers of enforcement, and any non-compliance has to be referred to the United Nations or the court's own oversight and legislative body, the Assembly of States Parties.

Of the six verdicts rendered by ICC, four were convicted as mentioned earlier. But it took the cooperation of their governments to bring them to justice. In the case of Duterte, it would be virtually impossible for the Philippine government to turn him over to ICC. So why even file a complaint against him?

While Duterte is safe from ICC prosecution for as long as he remains on Philippine soil, he can be served an ICC arrest warrant in another country where he may be visiting, provided that country is a signatory to the Rome Statute and would cooperate with the ICC, as in the case of Jean-Pierre Bemba Gombo.

At the end of the day, the ICC case against of Duterte, while it may seem like an exercise in futility, would bring the killings to the consciousness of the international community who can then use political pressure and economic sanctions including the freezing of foreign bank accounts of Duterte and his company.

Ooooo

9
Did Xi Take Trump for a Ride

May 23, 2017

When President Donald Trump met his Chinese counterpart Xi Jinping at his luxurious resort Mar-a-Lago in Palm Beach, Florida last April 6, he was hoping that Xi would accept his invitation to stay at the posh resort. Well, Xi politely declined and instead stayed at a nearby hotel. But other than that, their summit was deemed a "success." Trump got something of geopolitical value that he thought would solve his North Korea dilemma. And Xi got something of great economic value that he coveted so much. But how do you measure who got more? It's like comparing apples and oranges, right?

After the recent Trump-Xi summit at Mar-a-Lago in Florida, Trump's hard-line stance against China melted like a marshmallow over a fire. After two days of negotiations, Trump declared that China was not a "currency manipulator" and decided to maintain the status quo on trade issues. That's a 180-degree turnaround from his position during the presidential campaign.

When Xi went back home, he ordered shipments of coal from North Korea to be turned back. Trump was ebullient when he got the news. He said that China took a "big step" in easing tensions between the two countries. He described his relationship with Xi as one with "good chemistry" and praised Xi for banning North Korean coal.

South Korea's new president Moon Jae-in and North Korean "supreme leader" Kim Jong-un.

But what has that to do with the North Korea "nuclear" problem? North Korea continues her nuclear program including developing intercontinental ballistic missiles (ICBMs) that could reach the U.S. Since the Trump-Xi summit, North Korea had attempted to launch ballistic missiles but failed when the missiles exploded in flight. The following day that South Korea elected Moon Jae-In as president, North Korea launched another missile test. It was successful. This led Moon to comment that war with North Korea was a "high possibility."

"Nuclear card"

Meanwhile, the situation in the South China Sea (SCS) has drastically changed: China put militarization of the region in high gear. In an attempt to please – or appease – China, Trump isn't doing anything. He even turned down three requests from the Pacific Fleet to conduct freedom of navigation operations (FONOPs) with 12 miles of China's militarized islands in the Spratlys. And in an act of arrogance, China's ambassador to the U.S. demanded that Trump remove the Commander of the U.S. Pacific Command, Admiral Harry Harris Jr., who has been a strong proponent of FONOP. But what reportedly irked China was when Harris called China "aggressive," saying the country does not "seem to respect the international agreements they've signed." He was referring to the Permanent Court of Arbitration (PCA) ruling that rejected China's "nine-dash line" claim, which covered 80% of the SCS.

North Korea's recent test launch of new ballistic missile Hwasong-12, which North Korea claims could reach the U.S.

Evidently, Xi has put Trump on ice by playing the North Korea "nuclear card." In other words, North Korea can now pursue her nuclear program, knowing that Trump wouldn't do anything to stop her for as long as Xi pursues the "denuclearization" of the Korean Peninsula. But for North Korea watchers, denuclearization is not going to happen because China wouldn't allow it to happen. If China wanted it to happen, she could have done it long time ago.

Another thing that's not going to happen is Korean reunification. If reunification were going to happen, it would be under a democratic government and China wouldn't allow that to happen.

Indeed, a divided Korea — with North Korea possessing nuclear weapons — would serve as a security buffer between China and the U.S. forces stationed just south of the demilitarized zone (DMZ). But if the North Korean communist government collapses and the Korean Peninsula is reunified under the South Korea government, China will lose a strategic advantage over the western part of the Sea of Japan; thus, giving South Korea and Japan full control of the Sea of Japan. This would allow South Korea and Japan to block the Korea Strait – which connects the Sea of Japan and the East China Sea (ECS) – if hostility with China erupts.

Senkaku Islands.

It's important to note that ECS is a hotly disputed region between China and Japan. The dispute is about ownership of the Senkaku Islands, a group of eight uninhabited isles and islets administered by Japan but contested by China. The sea's strategic value is important to China because it connects to the SCS through the Taiwan Strait. To the east of the ECS is the Ryukyu archipelago, which is Japanese territory and to the west is China.

Arbitral tribunal

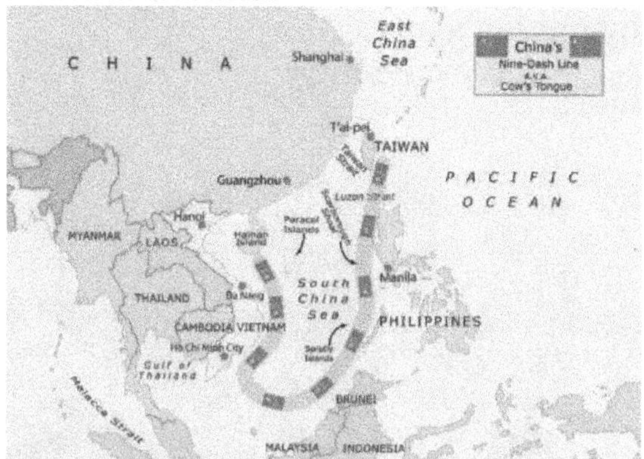

Nine-dash line.

This brings us back to the SCS, which China claims by virtue of the "nine-dash line," an arbitrary line that demarcates 80% of the South China Sea. But last July, the Permanent Court of Arbitration (PCA) in The Hague, Netherlands, issued a ruling in the Republic of the Philippines vs. People's Republic of China that invalidates the "nine-dash line," thus rendering China's claim null and void. Beijing immediately rejected the PCA's ruling.

Meanwhile, the newly elected President Rodrigo Duterte of the Philippines, who was sworn into office just 12 days prior to the PCA tribunal award, had a different idea. Instead of pursuing the PCA's award, he "temporarily" set it aside. During an event at the *Libingan ng mga Bayani* (Heroes' Cemetery), Duterte told Chinese Ambassador Zhao Jinhua that he does not want to go to war with China. Duterte then proposed that both the Philippines and China should just have a "soft landing everywhere." After Duterte's decision to set the tribunal award temporarily, China showered the Philippines with financial loans.

Rude awakening

Xi Jinping asked the PLA to be ready for a "regional war." (File Photo: September 2014).

Last May 15, Duterte met with Chinese President Xi Jinping during the "One Belt, One Road" summit in Beijing. Duterte told Xi, *"We intend to drill oil there, if it's yours, well, that's your view, but my view is I can drill the oil, if there is some inside the bowels of the earth, because it is ours."* Xi responded, saying: **"Well, if you force this, we'll be forced to tell you the truth. We will go to war. We will fight you."**

It must have been a rude awakening for Duterte who had called Xi a "great president." "China loves the Philippines and the Filipino people," Duterte once said of his new friend Dand idol. Who would go to war with a friend? Clearly, things have changed, which begs the question: Why the direct and undiplomatic verbal assault on Duterte?

Xi knows that Duterte is weak – very weak – who by his own admission said *"We cannot stop China from doing its thing. What do you want me to do? Declare war against China? I can, but we'll lose all our military and policemen tomorrow!"* If Xi uses Sun Tzu's *"Art of War"* tactics, he knows that not only Duterte is weak; U.S. President Donald Trump is weak, too. And this raises the question: Would Trump honor the U.S.-Philippines Mutual Defense Treaty (MDT) if Duterte invoked it? If no, then the Philippines would be helplessly at the mercy of China. And for as long as Xi keeps promising Trump that he's working to denuclearize the Korean Peninsula, Trump would remain neutral in the territorial disputes in the SCS.

When Xi warned Duterte, "We will go to war," he knew exactly what Duterte would do: Withdraw. And if Duterte has the cojones to proceed drilling for oil, what would Xi do? Would he ask Trump to rein in Duterte just like when Trump asked Xi to rein in North Korea's "supreme leader," Kim Jong-un?

Indeed, any way it's played out, Xi wins. He keeps North Korea nuclear-armed and the South China Sea in his possession. Which makes one wonder: Did Xi take Trump for a ride when they met at Mar-a-Lago?

Ooooo

10
Trump's 'House of Cards'

May 15, 2017

On the day of Donald J. Trump's presidential inauguration, a trailer of Season 5 of the "House of Cards" Netflix series was shown. The trailer – which movie critics dubbed "creepy" – accompanied an upside down American flag, along with the tweet: *"We make terror."* This line is a recall of last season's final episode, when Underwood said, *"We don't submit to terror. We make the terror."*

I am not trying to promote the controversial series but I can't help but notice the stark similarities between Trump and President Francis J. Underwood, the villainous character in the "House of Cards." Sometimes it makes me wonder whether Trump is play-acting the role of the scheming and wily Underwood or Underwood is playing the real-life Trump.

It seems like the producers are going to take "House of Cards" to a level that would parallel the Trumpian presidency – with all the intrigues, lies, corruption, dirt, and warts that would make Underwood look like an altar boy. Yes, Season 5 will be all about Trump masquerading as Underwood. It would be Trump's "House of Cards."

Trump and Francis J. Underwood, plays U.S. president in the Netflix series "House of Cards."

For starters, the similarity of personality between Trump and Underwood makes people wonder if the presidency is no longer the domain of statesmen who are more concerned about policy rather than politics. Gone are the days when the nation's elected leaders brought honor to the presidency. Trump, in the first 100 days of his presidency has dragged the office to a level of disrespect not seen before. Indeed, his first acts as president created chaos, which set the tone of how he is going to run the government for the next four years.

Assault on women

Women protesting Trump's assault on women.

But if the first week of Trump's presidency was a precursor of what it would be like in the next 200 weeks, then the American people should be prepared to ride a roller coaster endlessly. Indeed, Trump did not disappoint them when the day after his inauguration, hundreds of thousands of women gathered in Washington to express their disgust over Trump's misogynistic behavior against women. In cities across the country, hundreds of thousands more converged on the streets in a show of solidarity.

Indeed, like Underwood, Trump's attitude on women smacks of the demeaning – and brutal — treatment of women during the dark ages. And this is manifested in his attempt to repeal the Affordable Care Act or "Obamacare" and replace it with a healthcare system that is deemed as an assault on women's health. With a majority of Americans expressing their opposition to *"Trumpcare,"* Trump demonstrated his cold-blooded persona by ignoring the nation's cry for compassion for the tens of millions who would be denied health coverage under Trumpcare, mostly women and the poor. Which makes one wonder: What is the underlying reason for Trump's obsession to repeal Obamacare and replace it with his own creation?

Trumpkenstein.

His first executive order – on Inauguration Day – involved "minimizing the economic burden" of Obamacare. But if there is one thing that's has emerged in his brazen experimentation of the people's healthcare is that he has created a Frankenstein… or should I say, Trumpkenstein?

Assault on immigrants

Americans protesting Trump's assault on immigrants.

While it's bad enough that creating Trumpkenstein is awfully insensitive, Trump's assault on immigrants – particularly those who are from certain Middle East countries – is repugnant and bespeaks of his anti-immigrant and anti-Muslim sentiment, which is driven by his "white nationalist" and anti-immigration xenophobia. The fact that he hired Steve Bannon – an avowed "white nationalist" with racist predisposition – to be his senior strategist and advisor, shows his disdain for people of color. Bannon, formerly the power behind the right-wing Breitbart News website, was the author of Trump's controversial travel ban executive orders.

A week after his inauguration, Trump signed the executive order "Protecting the Nation from Foreign Terrorist Entry into the United States," the so-called "Travel Ban." However, immigration advocates call it more aptly, "Muslim Ban." When the Federal Court stopped its implementation, Trump revised it to make it more legally "palatable." But once again the Federal Court rejected it. It is now on appeal.

"Golden Visas" for sale

Jared Kushner's father Charles Kushner and sister Nicole Meyer and a rendering on One Journal Square building they're trying to fund with the sale of "Golden Visas" to wealthy Chinese investors.

But while the travel ban restricts, if not prohibits, the issuance of visas to people from seven predominantly Muslim countries, a scandal erupted recently involving Trump's family. It was revealed in the media that Trump's senior adviser and son-in-law Jared Kushner's family real estate business, "The Kushner Companies" – which holds around 20,000 apartments and 13 million square feet of commercial space across the U.S. — is involved in promoting a program that would allow wealthy foreigners in obtaining EB-5 Investor Visas, pejoratively called "Golden Visas."

A wide screen image showing a juxtaposition of Kushner1 project and President Trump displayed behind the podium where Nicole Meyer is making a project presentation.

Recently, Jared's sister Nicole Kushner Meyer organized an event in Beijing to lure 300 wealthy Chinese to invest a total of $150 million in a 79-story apartment building in New Jersey called Kushner 1. Marketing materials distributed by Nicole cited the Kushner family's "celebrity" status. Although the White House said that Jared has no involvement in the project, the family's relationship with Trump was highlighted when a wide screen image showing a juxtaposition of the project and President Trump was displayed behind the podium. Like they say, "A picture is worth a thousand words." Yes, indeed.

Surmise it to say, if the name-dropping and showing of Trump's image on the wall was intended to attract and influence people to invest, then one can say that such ploy is tantamount to "influence peddling," which constitutes corruption. And by the way, during the marketing presentation, journalists were asked to leave the room.

Abuse of power

Trump meets Russia's Foreign Minister Sergey Lavrov (left) and Ambassador to the U.S. Sergey Kislyak (right) in the Oval Office.

Trump promised to "drain the swamp" at the nation's capital, but instead he raised the level of corruption, which has become a trademark of the Trump presidency. And then there is also the alleged collusion between the Trump campaign and Russia to hack the U.S. elections in favor of Trump, who won the presidency by garnering a majority of the Electoral College votes. However, he lost the popular vote to Hillary Clinton by more than three million votes. While this quirk in the political system had happened a few times in the past due mainly to the way the Electoral College votes were distributed, Trump's victory is being questioned by many people who blamed Russia's alleged hacking had changed the calculus of the election results.

To date, the FBI investigation into possible Trump-Russia collusion has caused heads to fall. The first was acting Attorney General Sally Yates whom Trump fired after she warned the White House about former National Security Adviser Gen. Michael Flynn's questionable contacts with some high Russian officials. Consequently, Trump fired Flynn. And then there was Congressman Jason Chaffetz, Chairman of the House Oversight and Government Reform Committee, who was torn between loyalty to the Republican Party and to his duty as "ethics watchdog." Faced with a lose-lose dilemma, he resigned from his congressional seat.

Last May 9, Trump fired FBI Director James Comey. According to Comey, he was fired because: (1) He never provided Trump with any assurance of personal loyalty, and (2) The FBI's investigation into possible Trump team collusion with Russia in the 2016 election was accelerating. And to complicate things, Deputy Attorney General Rod Rosenstein reportedly threatened to quit after he was named as the "driving force" – which he denied — behind Trump's decision to fire Comey.

There were two collateral damages to the Trump-Russia collusion investigation. The first was Attorney General Jeff Sessions who recused himself from the investigation. And the second was Congressman Devin Nunes who recused himself as Chairman of the House Intelligence Committee after he announced that he was under investigation by the House Committee on Ethics because of public reports that he "may have made unauthorized disclosures of classified information."

Angela Reid, former White House Usher fired by Trump without any explanation.

Unrelated to the Trump-Russia investigation, Trump fired another Federal employee: Angela Reid, former White House Usher. No reason was given for the firing of Reid who was a native of Jamaica. But what is glaringly apparent is that Reid is a woman, an immigrant, and a person of color! Did Trump fire her because she didn't fit into the "white nationalist" crowd that he surrounds himself with in the White House?

With all these people being fired or resigning from the government, it makes one wonder if the "House of Cards" that Trump built on lies, intrigues, and deceit would survive public scrutiny.

Ooooo

11
Vietnam: Uncle Sam's Newest Ally?

June 14, 2017

South Vietnamese general shoots suspected Viet Cong official in the head. (Ed Adams/AP).

Once enemies, the U.S. and Vietnam have become friends over the course of four decades. While it did not happen overnight, what transpired was a slow process of rapprochement between the two countries. It took two generations of Vietnamese and Americans to set aside the bitterness they both have on each other. Why not?

More than 58,000 American and 282,000 South Vietnamese soldiers were killed from 1955 to 1975. North Vietnam and the Viet Cong suffered 444,000 military casualties and 627,000 civilian deaths.

Last day of Vietnam War: South Vietnamese fleeing from the North Vietnamese try to get into a U.S. Marine helicopter on top of a tower at the U.S. Embassy in Saigon.

After the fall of Saigon, tens of thousands of South Vietnamese civilians and former soldiers fled the country. Known as "boat people," the refugees used boats of all sizes to escape the North Vietnamese communists. They migrated to other countries, in particular the nearby Philippines where the government resettled them. However, the U.S. was their country of choice; thus, the process of looking for sponsors began. American families opened their homes and welcomed them. Eventually, most of them were able to find jobs and own their homes. Over time, the Vietnamese immigrants were allowed to petition for family members provided that they have jobs and financial capability to put them up. By 2014, 1.3 million Vietnamese immigrants resided in the U.S.

Beyond the strong affinity displayed by the Vietnamese people toward their former enemies, government-to-government relations between the U.S. and Vietnam improved considerably.

Cultural and economic ties progressed at a pace that surpassed the most optimistic expectations.

Obama and Vietnam

President Barack Obama and his Vietnamese counterpart Truong Tan Sang shake hands at their meeting in Washington, DC.

On July 25, 2013, the historic meeting between President Barack Obama and his Vietnamese counterpart Truong Tan Sang in Washington, DC broke new ground in U.S.-Vietnam bilateral relations. Obama and Truong decided to form a U.S.-Vietnam Comprehensive Partnership, which underlined the principles of *"respect for the U.N. Charter, international law, and each other's political systems, independence, sovereignty, and territorial integrity."* The two leaders pledged that their countries would continue to cooperate on defense and security matters.

On May 23, 2016, Obama visited Hanoi and announced that the U.S. would fully lift a longstanding embargo on lethal arms sale to Vietnam, a decision that may have been precipitated by China's military build-up in the South China Sea (SCS). Obama said that the lifting of the arms embargo *"will ensure Vietnam has access to the equipment it needs to defend itself and removes a lingering vestige of the Cold War."*

Trump and Vietnam

President Donald Trump and Vietnamese Prime Minister Nguyen Xuan Phuc shake hands at their meeting in Washington, DC.

Recently, Vietnamese Prime Minister Nguyen Xuan Phuc visited President Donald J. Trump in the White House. His visit is significant because there have been perceptions that Vietnam was leaning to China, and the U.S. is veering away from the Indo-Asia-Pacific region. This caused many countries in the region – including Vietnam and the Philippines – to move closer to China. The leaders of the other eight ASEAN countries are adjusting their alignment as well. They're preparing themselves in the event that Trump would leave the region altogether.

But the U.S. visit of Nguyen has changed all that. Nguyen was the first ASEAN leader to visit Washington, DC since Trump was inaugurated president. With the meeting of Trump and Nguyen in the White House on May 31, it was evident that Trump is not reversing the course of

U.S. policy in the Indo-Asia-Pacific region. The "Pivot to Asia" that Obama started may have changed in name, but the objectives are the same: to protect U.S. interests in the Indo-Asia-Pacific region.

The meeting between the two leaders produced a joint statement to "Enhance the Comprehensive Partnership between the U.S. and Vietnam." Their joint statement reiterates that the *"United States is a 'Pacific power with widespread interests and commitments throughout the Asia Pacific.' It maintains all elements of the U.S.-Vietnam Comprehensive Partnership that was established during the Obama administration. It goes a step further, stating that President Trump and Prime Minister [Nguyen] Phuc are committed to making the partnership 'deeper, more substantive, and more effective.' For the first time the two former enemies stress at the summit level their 'pledge to strengthen cooperation in the fields of security and intelligence.' "*

Which makes one wonder: Is this just another diplomatic hyperbole or does it seem like it would lead to stronger defense and economic ties between the two countries?   While a defense treaty would not be politically feasible at this time as it would certainly irk China and would also affect Vietnamese-Russian security relations, an arrangement similar to the U.S.-India Logistics Exchange Memorandum of Agreement (LEMOA) just might do the work. But while LEMOA might fall short of a "basing agreement," it gives the militaries of both countries access to each other's facilities for supplies and repair. It's a good start that could lead to a *de facto* – if not official – defense arrangement.

With this new U.S.-Vietnam Enhanced Comprehensive Partnership, the two countries would be able to deter China's aggressive behavior in the SCS; thus, protect Vietnam's EEZ from Chinese encroachment. Indeed, what is at stake is Vietnam's economic interest in the SCS.

Defense cooperation and the SCS issue were prominently addressed in the joint statement. Trump and Nguyen affirmed that the SCS is a "waterway of strategic significance." They also discussed the possibility of a visit to a Vietnamese port – Cam Ranh Bay — by a U.S. aircraft carrier and steps to further cooperation between their two naval forces.

Vietnam will never forget the Battle of the Paracel Islands in 1974 when China occupied the islands, which are claimed by Vietnam. Vietnam attempted to expel the Chinese Navy from the vicinity. A battle ensued and the Chinese forces prevailed. China established *de facto* control over the Paracels. However, Vietnam maintained her claim over the Paracels to this day.

A "first" in U.S.-Vietnam relations

China deploys giant oil rig in the waters near the Paracel Islands.

In 2014, China deployed her biggest oil rig into Vietnam's exclusive economic zone (EEZ). Vietnam then sent to the U.S. her number two man on the ruling Politburo, Executive Secretary of the Communist Party of Vietnam Dinh The Huynh. That was a "first" in U.S.-Vietnam relations.

Indeed, for the most part of the last two decades, the Philippines and Singapore led the rest of ASEAN in engaging the U.S. With the rift that Philippine President Rodrigo Duterte has with the U.S., the Philippines has cocooned herself into isolation. With the vacuum created by the Philippines, Vietnam would be more than willing to play a key role in engagement with the U.S.

U.S. donates six coastal patrol boats to Vietnam.

As a sign of closer U.S.-Vietnam military ties, the U.S. transferred six patrol boats to the Vietnam Coast Guard last May. The U.S. embassy released a statement, which said, *"The handover represented deepening cooperation to maritime law enforcement and humanitarian assistance in Vietnam's territorial waters and exclusive economic zone."*

U.S. Secretary of Defense James Mattis (5th L) poses for a picture with ASEAN defense leaders after a meeting on the sidelines of the 16th IISS Shangri-La Dialogue in Singapore, June 4, 2017.

At the recently concluded Shangri-La Dialogue in Singapore, U.S. Defense Secretary James Mattis said during his address to some 500 delegates: *"The US can't accept Chinese actions that impinge on the interests of the international community, undermining the rules-based order that has benefited all countries represented here today including, and especially, China."* He added that while conflict with China is not "inevitable," the two countries will engage in competition. And that's where Uncle Sam needs reliable allies to compete with China, which begs the question: Is Vietnam emerging as Uncle Sam's newest ally in the Indo-Asia-Pacific region?

(PerryDiaz@gmail.com)

Ooooo

12
Trump's Gunboat Diplomacy

June 7, 2017

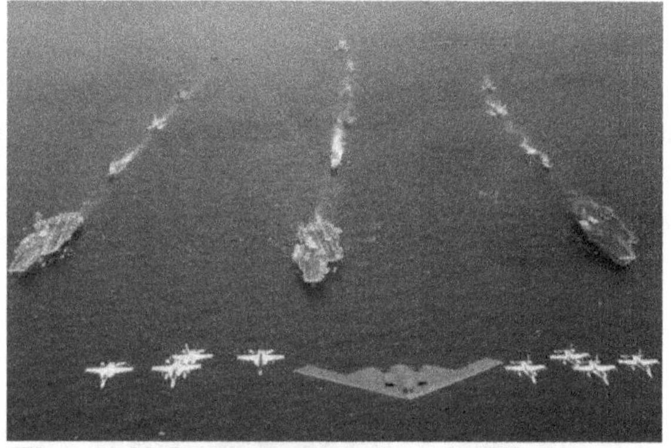

Three U.S. supercarrier battle groups sail in formation.

In my column, *"China's gunboat diplomacy"* (July 19, 2012), I wrote: " 'China frigate leaves shoal: [Malacañang] Palace happy,' said a huge electronic billboard, which I saw on the way to the Ninoy Aquino International Airport to catch a plane home last July 16, 2012. The news of a grounded guided missile Chinese frigate near Half Moon Shoal (Hasa-Hasa Shoal) in the Spratly archipelago, 69 miles west of Palawan, raised the tension level between the Philippines and China ever since the latter declared the entire West Philippine Sea (South China Sea) an extension of her territorial continental shelf in 2010. And China made it crystal clear that this vast body of water — rich in *oil and natural gas deposits — is a 'core national interest,' which in diplomatic parlance means 'non-negotiable.'*

"And to make sure that everybody — including the United States — knows that she is serious about her stand on the issue, China is building a naval force that would make her the dominant sea power in Asia-Pacific by 2020. And to let everybody know that she means business, she acquired an old aircraft carrier from Russia and retrofitted it with state-of-the-art technology and is now undergoing sea trials."

Floating airbases

New supercarrier USS Gerald R. Ford.

With 10 operational supercarriers and a new one — the USS Gerald R. Ford — joining the fleet in a few months, that means that the U.S. could deploy up to six carrier battle groups to cover the entire Indo-Asia-Pacific region. In addition to these supercarriers, the U.S. has nine amphibious assault ships that are more like aircraft carriers on a smaller scale.

Although China is way behind in her aircraft carrier-building program, she has now two carriers. The first one, a refurbished Cold War-era Russian carrier, is barely operational and the second – which was her first to build indigenously

— is currently undergoing sea trials before she's commissioned for deployment. With a 10 to one ratio in favor of the U.S., the Chinese Navy wouldn't stand a chance against America's large fleet of supercarriers.

USS Langley (CV-1), the first aircraft carrier built in 1920.

Ever since the U.S. converted the collier USS Jupiter into an aircraft carrier — the USS Langley (CV-1) — in 1920, the U.S. became the world's dominant naval power because of her ability to deploy aircraft to these floating airbases at sea. Consequently, two more colliers were converted into aircraft carriers. After that, the U.S. built six brand-new aircraft carriers. By the time World War II erupted, America had the naval advantage no other world power had.

Big Stick ideology

Big Stick ideology.

With the capability to project air power in the high seas, the U.S. pursued her foreign policy objectives with what had come to be known as "gunboat diplomacy" or "Big Stick ideology." In other words, the conspicuous display of naval power anywhere in the world implies a direct threat of warfare, which forces another country to agree to terms America demands.

In World War II, the U.S. was able to defeat the Japanese naval forces in the Pacific because of the use of aircraft carriers. Had Japan destroyed America's aircraft carrier fleet based at Pearl Harbor in 1942, the outcome of the Pacific war might have been different. Fortunately, due to intelligence reports of an impending Japanese sneak attack on Pearl Harbor, the U.S. moved her entire aircraft carrier fleet out of harm's way into the open sea.

During the Cold War, the U.S. started building large nuclear-powered aircraft carriers that came to be known as "supercarriers." Following the new 100,000-ton Gerald R. Ford-class (CVN-78) of supercarriers, two others — the USS John F. Kennedy (CVN-79) and USS

Enterprise (CVN-80) — are in various stages of construction.

Clinton's gunboat diplomacy

Taiwan Strait.

On July 21, 1995, the People's Republic of China (PRC) triggered what is called the 1995-1996 Taiwan Strait Crisis. That was when she fired a series of missile "tests" in the waters surrounding the Republic of China (ROC) – commonly known as Taiwan. It was believed that the first set of missiles was intended to send a "strong signal" to the Lee Teng-hui's government, who was perceived as moving the ROC's foreign policy away from the "One-China Policy." The second set of missiles was fired in early 1996. It was believed that it was intended to intimidate the Taiwanese voters in the run-up of the 1996 presidential election.

In March 1996, with the threat of PRC invasion, President Bill Clinton ordered the deployment of two supercarrier battle groups – the USS Nimitz and USS Independence – to the region. The Nimitz and the amphibious assault ship USS Belleau Wood daringly sailed through the Taiwan Strait, the narrow channel that separates the PRC from Taiwan. Unable to respond to the Nimitz's "provocation," the PRC realized then that she couldn't stop the U.S. from coming to the aid of Taiwan, and the PRC humiliatingly backed off.

Since then, the PRC embarked on a massive build-up of her naval forces. But today, she is still short of catching up to America's naval prowess. However, with more than a thousand land-based missiles deployed along China's coast facing Taiwan, China might be bold enough to respond next time the U.S. deploys a carrier battle group to the Taiwan Strait.

North Korea problem

North Korea launches multiple test missiles.

Recently, North Korea took a big step in the development of intercontinental ballistic missiles (ICBMs). She is also believed to possess of more than a dozen nuclear warheads that can be delivered by ICBMs, which would make the U.S. vulnerable to North Korean nuclear attack. It couldn't be ascertained if they're already operational. However, at the rate North Korea has been conducting missile tests, which seem to be successful, it would just be a matter of time before she becomes a threat to America's security.

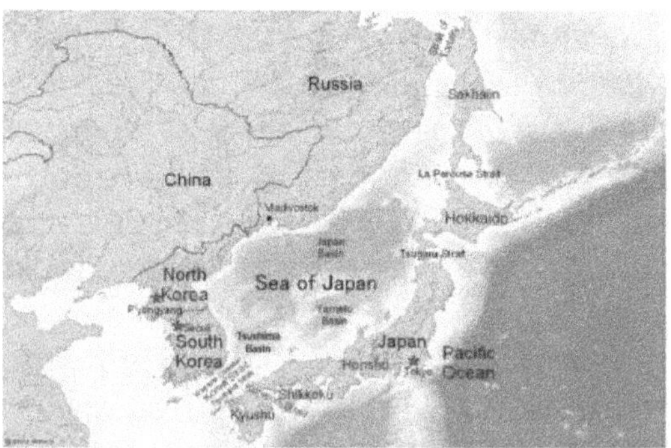

Sea of Japan.

In a move reminiscent of the 1995-1996 Taiwan Crisis, the Trump administration deployed two carrier battle groups – the USS Ronald Reagan and USS Carl Vinson — to the Sea of Japan, which is within striking distance of North Korea.

In addition to the two battle groups, the USS Nimitz has been ordered to deploy to the Western Pacific to join the other two carrier battle groups. The deployment of Nimitz marks a rare situation, when a total of three carrier battle groups are simultaneously deployed in one region. Some analysts say that the Nimitz's deployment might be a "special contingency plan." With four to five guided missile cruisers and destroyers and one or two nuclear attack submarines accompanying each supercarrier, the large assemblage of naval assets in a theater of operations has never been bigger since the end of World War II.

There has been a lot of speculation about what's in President Donald Trump's mind when he allowed three carrier battle groups to converge in waters near North Korea. In a recent telephone conversation between Philippine President

Rodrigo Duterte, Trump told Duterte: *"We have two submarines — the best in the world. We have two nuclear submarines, not that we want to use them at all."* In response to news report of their conversation, North Korean officials said that their country was ready for nuclear attacks in the event of "U.S. military aggression."

With the White House loaded with retired military generals whom Trump has given a lot of latitude to decide what military action to take when the need arises, there are two ways this situation could lead to. One would be to use the template of Clinton's "gunboat diplomacy" during the 1995-1996 Taiwan Strait Crisis that could compel North Korea to back off and sue for peace. If that is going to happen, then Trump's "gunboat diplomacy" works. However, if North Korea fights back with a nuclear attack on South Korea, then all hell breaks loose!

(PerryDiaz@gmail.com)

ooooo

13.
Uncle Sam or Xi Dada: A question of trust

February 15, 2017

American, German, and Japanese flags.

One of the most quoted maxims in politics is: "There are no permanent friends, no permanent enemies, only permanent interests." But regardless of whether you're dealing with a friend or an enemy, the one that could earn dividends is the mantra: "Don't burn your bridges because you'll never know when you would need them." American presidents since the beginning of the 19th century were good at following this mantra. Not only did they not burn bridges, they built bridges for their former enemies. Yes, indeed. Look at post-World War II Germany and Japan.

At the end of World War II, the U.S. initiated the Marshall Plan – officially the European Recovery Program – to aid Western Europe from the ravages of war. More than $12 billion (approximately $120 billion in current dollar value) were given in the 1950s and 1960s. The reunification of West Germany and the former communist state of East Germany in 1990 created Europe's biggest economic power. Today, the U.S. continues to maintain a strong military force to protect Germany and 25 other European countries – collectively the North Atlantic Treaty Organization (NATO) — from the threat of Russian aggression.

In the case of Japan, the American occupation of Japan provided a smooth transition to economic recovery. With the presence of American bases and troops, Japan allocated only one percent of her Gross Domestic Product (GDP) for her self-defense force; thus, giving her more to spend on economic recovery. By the 1960s, Japan became the world's second largest economy after the U.S.

Today, Germany and Japan join the ranks of America's most dependable allies. Germany, together with her World War II adversaries — United Kingdom and France — form the bulwark of NATO while Japan partners with the U.S. and South Korea in keeping China and North Korea at bay.

Rise of China

With the rise of China as the world's second largest economy after the U.S. – displacing Japan who moved down to third place — there is a great deal of anxiety among her Asian neighbors who are fearful of China's imperialistic design in the South and East China Seas. Thus far, Vietnam and the Philippines have lost territories to China. In 1974, China grabbed the Paracel Islands after engaging Vietnam in a fierce naval battle. In 1994, China occupied the Mischief Reef, which is within the Philippines' exclusive economic zone (EEZ), and built permanent fortifications on it.

In 2012, China took possession of the Philippines' Scarborough Shoal after four months of standoff between Chinese and Philippine coast guards. To break the impasse, the U.S. mediated for both parties to withdraw their vessels from the shoal. Both countries agreed. Well, the Philippines withdrew her ships but China didn't. Since then, China cordoned the only opening to the shoal's lagoon; thus, preventing Philippine ships and fishing vessels from entering what was once Philippine territory.

In 2013, China started building artificial islands on seven reefs in the Spratly archipelago in the South China Sea (SCS). When the U.S. confronted China about those artificial islands, China said she had no intention of militarizing them. However, satellite photos show runways, harbors, and structures that appear to be missile emplacements. When asked again, China said that she has the right to build and install defense equipment on her sovereign territory.

Can China be trusted?

Reclaimed Fiery Cross Reef showing airfield, harbor, and buildings.

Chinese warplanes landed on Fiery Cross Reef.

The representations that China made when she was building the artificial islands were different from what she's saying now; she's fortifying these islands to defend them from external forces. It manifests China's propensity to lie. In other words, China can't be trusted.

In a survey conducted by Social Weather Stations (SWS) in the Philippines last September, 76% of the respondents had "much trust" in the

U.S. compared to 22% about China. What is interesting is that the survey was conducted at a time when Digong was vociferously expressing his anti-American tirades.

President Rodrigo Duterte giving the middle finger to the U.S.

Duterte continued his verbal assaults on the U.S., particularly against then-President Barack Obama whom he called "son of a whore" and told him to "go to hell." But Duterte seemed to be attracted to then President-elect Donald Trump who talked to him on the phone telling him that he was doing the "right thing" in his war on drugs.

As an expression of goodwill towards Trump, Duterte sent his Communications Secretary Martin Andanar and National Security Adviser Gen. Hermogenes Esperon to attend Trump's inaugural last January 20. Although there were no news reports of the two attending the inaugural ball and having a seat at the VIP section at the inauguration, they were at the pre-inaugural reception at the Philippine Embassy, which was mostly attended by Filipino-Americans.

Change in Duterte

A changed Duterte?

Something must have happened since then because Duterte seemed to have a change in his attitude towards Uncle Sam.

Recently, it was reported in the news that Duterte had given Defense Secretary Gen. Delfin Lorenzana the go-ahead for the U.S. military to build barracks and fuel depots in designated Philippine bases where American forces are allowed to temporarily station under the Enhanced Defense Cooperation Agreement (EDCA). This is a far cry from last month when Duterte threatened to terminate EDCA. He said then that he didn't want his country to get entangled if a Sino-American war erupted. Lorenzana identified three bases where the U.S. is supposedly bringing weapons, including Palawan, which is just within 100-200 miles from the militarized artificial islands in the Spratly archipelago in the SCS.

Realignment

CPP Chairman Jose Ma. Sison reacted to Duterte's lifting of the ceasefire with the New People's Army.

Obviously, Duterte is realigning with the U.S., just a few months after he announced during his state visit to China that he will "separate" from the U.S. His 180-degree about-face surprised the Duterte watchers.

Last February 5, Duterte announced that he had terminated the peace talks with leaders of the Communist Party of the Philippines (CPP) and the National Democratic Front (NDF). He also lifted the "ceasefire" with the New People's Army (NPA). In a media conference, Duterte said that the CPP-NDF-NPA triumvirate was making unreasonable demands including freeing hundreds of prisoners whom NPA claims to be "political prisoners." Duterte had initially released 18 prisoners but their number was increased to 23 upon the insistence. After releasing them, the rebels demanded the release of another 400 prisoners. It was then that Duterte ordered the arrest of jailed leftist leaders who were allowed to join the peace talks.

Duterte then branded the CPP-NDF-NPA as a terrorist group, which didn't dwell too well with Chinese President Xi Jinping. It's a big blow to Xi whom the Chinese people affectionately call Uncle Xi or *Xi Dada*. Xi had expected Duterte to turn the Philippines into a vassal of China and terminate EDCA including the Mutual Defense Treaty (MDT) and Visiting Forces Agreement (VFA). And with a navy without warships and an air force without warplanes, the Philippines would helplessly be at the mercy of a militant China. What a shame!

At the end of the day, the defensive umbrella that Uncle Sam provides over the Philippines would ensure that the country remains sovereign and independent. Unlike Xi Dada, Uncle Sam has no imperialistic design in the Philippines. However, America has vast national security interests in the Indo-Asia-Pacific region and thus has to remain a power in the region to keep the strategic shipping lanes in the SCS and other bodies of international water open to all nations.

Ultimately, it all comes down to a question of trust. Whom can Duterte trust: Uncle Sam or Xi Dada.

Ooooo

14
Why I Publish/Reprint Books

Tatay Jobo Elizes
Self-Publisher

Writings are timeless and they act as mirrors to history. I publish writings as they remain relevant anytime. I have seen a lot of good writings in the internet, in magazines and newspapers. But most writers have only one or two articles and therefore not enough material to be published as a book. And yet, many of them need to be published or archived. There are also writers who write a lot but never publish them. There are also old books with no more prints available. The solution is to publish/reprint.

I do this for free because of the print-books-on-demand (POD) system, but the printed or hardcopy is not free

The printed book will always be there among your collections or libraries. Not all use the internet. The internet access has its technical problems. I can produce fiction, non-fiction, in color also.

My booklist can be seen at http://tinyurl.com/mj76ccq (copy and paste)

Permission had been granted by the author/ authors to print their books under my free self-publishing service. They own copyrights to their works.

Interested reader may request free reading of any of my books, articles or essays via online reading or ebook. Just email me.

Thank you.

ooooo